PASSIVE INCOME: STEP-BY-STEP GUIDE TO MAKE YOU EXPERT IN MAKING MONEY ONLINE.

Don't work for the money, let the money work for you.

I0504478

©By: Mohammad Alsafwani

Table of Contents

BLURB

I want to thank and congratulate you for purshising the book, *"Passive Income: Step-by-step guide to make you expert in making money online."*

This book contains proven steps and strategies when it comes to understanding of the facets of growing your passive income. The book tries to shed more insights on how to start a successful journey towards acuiring a stable stream of passive online income. Some of the mind-boggling ideas tackled here include blogging, e-commerce, affiliate marketing, Cryptocurrency trading and the likes.

If you have to live on a 9 to 5 job lifestyle, then you are in the right place to change this. The book gives you some excellent tips on how to turn the tables and leave a life free of budget constraints. Thanks again for purshising this book, I hope you enjoy it!

The information herein is offered for informational purposes solely, and is universal as so. The presentation of the information is without contract or any type of guarantee assurance.

The trademarks that are used are without any consent, and the publication of the trademark is without permission or backing by the trademark owner. All trademarks and brands within this book are for clarifying purposes only and are the owned by the owners themselves, not affiliated with this document.

Introduction

One of the keys to getting rich and creating wealth is to understand the different ways in which income can be generated. It's often said that the lower and middle-class work for money whilst the rich have money work for them. The key to wealth creation lies within this simple statement.

Imagine, rather than you working for money you instead made every dollar work for you 40hrs a week. Better still, imagine each and every dollar working for you 24/7 i.e. 168hrs/week. Figuring out the best ways you can make money work for you is an important step on the road to wealth creation.

Passive income is income generated from a trade or business, which does not require the earner to participate. It is often investment income (i.e. income that is not obtained through working) but not exclusively. The central tenet of this type of income is that it can expect to continue whether you continue working or not. As you near retirement you are most definitely seeking to replace earned income with passive, unearned income. The secret to wealth creation earlier on in life is passive income; positive cash-flow generated by assets that you control or own.

One of the reasons people find it difficult to make the leap from earned income to more passive sources of income is that the entire education system is actually pretty much designed to teach us to do a job and hence rely largely on earned income. This works for governments as this kind of income generates large volumes of tax but will not work for you if you're focus is on how to become rich and wealth building. However, to become rich and create wealth you will be re?uired to cross the chasm from relying on earned income only.

Chapter 1

Why A Passive Income Business Should Always Be The Additional Income Source

Everyone seems to be looking for an additional income source these days. Online passive income opportunities are certainly the most potential ventures for someone who's willing to add some extra cash to his account regularly. However, these passive income sources should only be taken as an additional income source, not the primary one. Here's why you should never consider a passive income generator as your primary source of income.

Why you shouldn't consider a passive income business as your primary income source?

A passive revenue business is the best way to supple your bank account without hampering your regular job or day-to-day business. However, this should never be taken the primary source or the only source. Else, you might face financial problems and instability. The reasons are explained here:

#1 No Limit (Minimum Or Maximum) Of Income

These passive income generators usually come with no guarantee or limit of income. This means, you cannot set a minimum or maximum threshold of income. So it will not be a realistic idea to use this income source as the primary financial source to manage and maintain your regular expenses. You definitely need to maintain a budget to carry out all those day to day expenses and those should be managed with a regular, definite income source.

#2 Saving Money As Your Retirement Plan

Experts always recommend saving some amount as a part of your retirement plan. The money you will be earning from a passive income generator should be saved as retirement funds. This will ensure your financial security for the future. You should save these extra cash for entertainments, retirement or even investments in future. This can only protect you money-wise and stable your personal finances.

#3 Passive Income Businesses Should Give You Extra Cash

The goal or perspective of a passive revenue opportunity is to make extra cash. This is the basic concept of making passive revenue. If you start depending on this, you might fail to pay your bills, repay your mortgage or maintain your other regular expenses. You should always avoid these situations and concentrate on a passive income generator as an additional monetary resource, nothing else!

#4 Don't Limit The Endless Potentials

The potentials of these passive income businesses are literally endless. You can make a huge cash with an effective, proven method. But taking this as your primary income source will ruin those potentials as you will be concentrating on a definite amount each month. As you will push hard to make certain amount of cash from the business, it will never uplift the resources to another level. That's why experts recommend these passive revenue generators to be added as a second income source so that you can make your personal finances even stronger.

There are several other reasons why you should never take a passive revenue opportunity as your bread-earner. Rather, you should move on and establish a business that makes you a definite sum to help you manage the day to day expenses.

Chapter 2

Top 10 Online Passive Income Ideas 2019

People are constantly seeking out ways to increase their earning and enjoy financial independence. Here I'm going to share the top 10 passive income ideas that made waves in 2018 and how you find passive income opportunities in those ideas in 2019.

The big question people often ask is whether one can live off their passive income earnings. If you work your passive income sources and build streams of residual income, you can get to the point where your passive income may equal what you are earning on your day job. And that is the goal, to build multiple streams of passive income so that it eventually equals or surpass what you are earning on your day job, at that point you may have been said to reach financial independence because then you have control of your time, your money is coming in to pay the bills even if you quit your main job and the system runs automatically, you just manage it.

I guess the question in your mind now is whether there is something you can do part time that will earn you almost a full-time income. Yes, there is, a matter of fact there are! Here we go with the top 10 passive income ideas of 2019

1.Affiliate marketing: affiliate marketing provides a fantastic opportunity for people who do not have a product of their own to take another person's good product and promote it at a profit on every sale they make. This is one of the easiest ways to start earning passive income.

2.eBook publishing: if you have an idea that can solve a specific problem, kindle publishing provides an easy way to put it in book form and publish it. Book publishing has never been so easy. A lot of persons have been asking if there is a business you can start with no money. This is one. Everything is free, if you can write your book, edit it, create an appealing cover and write a good description for your book, you can start earning money right away.

3.Cryptocurrency: cryptocurrency gained good attention in 2019 as a source of creating residual income. There are two ways basically for making money with cryptocurrency. That is trading and mining. The good thing about this system is that you can trade from your mobile.

4.Network marketing: network marketing or multi-level marketing is one of the oldest businesses around, a system where you start at the bottom and work your way to the top. Though the talk about multi-level marketing may not sound like a buzzword yet big companies have been using it to get hot products into the market and individuals have been using it to rise to great heights and earning both passive and massive income for themselves.

5.Freelancing: you have probably heard of websites like up work, fiver, elance and so on, where people go to get various kinds of digital work done for them. You too can start earning money right away if you have one of the skills that are required on daily basis from these websites e.g. writing articles, editing articles, book cover design, website development etc

6.Blogging: yes people are still earning from blogging even though the market seems to be saturated. There are more tools that make it easy for anybody to create a blog and take it to prominence. Blogging is a good way to start earning passive income but it's not the quickest way to build passive income. That being said, it is also important to note that it is one of the surest ways to build a reputation and a longer-lasting stream of residual income if you do it right.

7.E-commerce: this used to be for big companies but today anyone can set up an e-commerce shop and start selling digital products online with WordPress and woocommerce plugins.

8.Drop shipping: this has to do with selling physical products through well-established e-commerce platforms like Aliexpress and Amazon. You don't have to do any difficult work, just research the top-selling products and promote them on your custom built e-commerce shop that is linked to the main platform and have the product delivered by the company while you pick the profit.

9.Mobile apps: there are more smartphones than there are human beings on the earth today. And what powers these devices? Mobile apps. If you have an idea that can solve a problem then there is an opportunity here for you to earn residual income. You don't have to be a programmer to create a mobile app. You just have to come up with the idea and outsource the job to a programmer on one of the freelance websites mentioned earlier to get it created.

10.Video blogging: YouTube is now the second most popular website in the world. If you have flair for video, then there is an opportunity here for you to earn passive income. YouTube with its AdSense program and partners program allow creators of video content to earn on the platform.

These are the top ten passive income ideas that are currently trending. If you want to start earning passive online income this year then you may want to consider one of these as a starting point to build your residual income streams.

Anybody can start building wealth at anytime from anywhere today. All it takes is to have the right ideas and desire to take action on what you know or learn. You can start building your way up to financial freedom like many others have done. In this post are ideas that you can take action on right now to start building a system of financial freedom.

Chapter 3

Strategies Of Increasing Online Passive Income Earnings

People build websites to earn traffic and eventually revenue. Many website owners have tried to find ways to maximize their earnings with different tactics and strategies. Their websites provide information and also with each visitor that comes to their page, they earn passive income. This is passive because it builds up while you just let your website grow. These usually come in the form of advertisements that will earn you revenue. Here are strategies you should consider to get the most out of your passive income online! Remember, earning revenue through ads needs a carefully woven strategy.

Website Dynamics

If you want to earn passive income, you've got to pay attention to your website's design. You can't just pick a simple and generic layout to fit your theme or topic. You have to work with what becomes aesthetic and appealing to look at.

You should make sure the ads are incorporated to your website's design. You wouldn't want it to stand out too much! Adjust the colors around to fit your theme. People hate seeing cluttered advertisements lying around websites. Make sure that your advertisements are placed in the navigation or near the upper portion of your website. This will ensure that they will be seen at first glance. Grabbing the readers' attention is always a key aspect in a good website design.

Website Content

Website content is a very integral strategy to consider! Since some ads can reflect your content, you should have informative write-ups to feed the ads with relevant information. When thinking of an ideal strategy to draw in more revenue, you should craft your write-ups in ways that will allow your readers to be satisfied of the information. At the same time, they will be compelled to look for relevant sources that can enrich their knowledge.

Whenever you consider your content, you should always hold it at top priority. In fact, it drives your website. Always place content that gives your visitors direct answers. If they already know what they are looking for, they may want to enrich that knowledge. Satisfaction can lead them to trusting your site for more information. Once you help them get that through the ads that aid them, you have done your part well.

It takes a dynamic and content-driven website to help you increase your revenue. Make sure you provide what visitors want. These two simple strategies can make or break a website, knowing the short attention span of internet surfers! Keep an active mind so you can readily adjust your site to cater to your visitors' needs.

Chapter 4

How to Create Online Passive Income Using BUM Marketing

BUM marketing has been around for many years, it's a relatively easier way for marketers to generate online revenues, this method has been proven to be effective. With the recent widely spread of the implementation of such method, more and more marketers has started making used of it to increase their online sales, even beginners finds it easy to apply. So what exactly bum marketing is, and how you can generate passive income from it?

The essence of bum marketing is by posting articles to directories, from there, the articles reader will be guided to visit a website, hence creating free traffic source. Every marketer knows that traffic is the most crucial part ensuring the success of their online business, and this is the area where most beginners find it challenging and often fail to accomplish which subsequently will force them to give up their initial intention of creating passive income streams online. But with bum marketing, the issue of getting traffic is greatly eliminated as soon one will find that after setting it up, the continuous traffic generated in months to come will definitely generate revenues from their website.

To start with, you will need to identify the type of traffic you want to generate, this simply means knowing exactly who your targeted visitors will be. Doing correctly this part is extremely important as it will determine if the visitors you are drawing to will eventually turn into buyers. In the online world, identifying visitors means identifying the right keyword, which is word phrase used by online users to search for information. For example, if some one is searching on 'free software', it implies this person are not ready to make any purchases as he is looking for free stuff, but if some one search on 'software discount', then very likely he is going to buy something. In identifying a right keyword, free keywords tools such as Google AdWords Keyword External Tool and Free WordTracker Keyword Tools comes in very handy, these tools provide information on what are the search terms used by online users, as well as many people are searching using such terms. The goal here is to look for keywords with high search volume, but yet less websites are ranked for that particular keywords, thus low competition for your article to ranked high in the search engines.

Once you have found your keywords, the next step is to create articles that contains these keywords, at the end of the article, you should provide a link to your web site. Once it has been created, then all you need to do is to submit it to various articles directories. There are so many article directories e.g standupwrite, article dashboard, articlecity etc. These articles directories are known to have high readership and there articles often get high rank in search engines such as Google. Once your article ranked high on search engine, you are ready to get visitors that will contribute to your online passive income!

Chapter 5

FAP Turbo and Forex Trading - Great Source of Extra Passive Income

Forex trading is a great source of income for anyone. However, it requires a lot of time, making it very difficult for people who have another job to succeed in this industry. Having a trading robot like FAP Turbo will help you have better results, and will dramatically decrease the amount of time that you need to spend in order to make money online. It automates almost 90% of the tasks, making Forex trading a great source of passive income.

Passive income grows automatically and most of the time, all you have to do is to spend the money. That is the reason why a lot of people are using trading robots with their trades. They want to automate their trading campaign allowing them to have more time with their families and friends. FAP Turbo is one of the few trading robots that can deliver great results and does not require human assistance.

FAP Turbo works on full automation, and is self-sustaining. This robot can even make decisions on its own making it a more preferable tool for most traders. It has been constantly delivering more than 95% profitable trades for the last 10 years, with an average of 4000% net profit every year. Most users are even saying that, with the help of FAP Turbo, they are making money from Forex trading without doing anything.

Using FAP Turbo with your trades is really a great source of passive income online. However, you should also understand that it will only happen if you have done your job of regularly updating the database of this robot, and studying the market in order to enhance your trading style, which will be used as the basis of the strategies executed by FAP Turbo.

Chapter 6

AdSense Money Maker - Let Google Be Your Source of Monthly Passive Income Long Term!

The internet is full of ads to make money from websites these days. One of the great method to make money online is with AdSense Money Maker.

Google AdSense is a very famous advertising network which is a paid-per-click program. It does not require any formal education or professional experience to do it. Many people are already successfully making money using AdSense Money Maker. It just requires you to copy and paste the code in your website.

You must have seen all over the internet few ads depicted successful stories of people who make several thousands in a very short period spending just few hours each day. Most of them are fake and do not blindly follow those stories. Of course, it is possible to make more money with AdSense but it involves spending lot of time each day in building sites and marketing them to grow their business.

Moreover, since Google is a reputable company, people just take up the AdSense program hoping to make more money while having belief in the credentials of the company while these advertising cheaters fill their wallets. AdSense Money Maker by Google is a very good way to make money from your website but you have to adopt to it full time. The income which you derive is passive and you can't see ⍰uicker results.

The secret to making money with this kind of pay-per-click advertising network is to drive traffic to your website. Depending on the amount of traffic your website gets, you make money. If those visiting your websites click on more ads, then you make more money. For this, first you need to learn how to drive traffic to your website. Since AdSense money maker requires you to set and leave it, your earnings will be reflected as and when you make money and it will come automatically.

Working with Google AdSense does not require highly educated qualifications. Instead any regular person can copy and paste the code which is provided by Google in their website and you will have to wait. The AdSense money maker works in the background making pennies and it takes time to build to larger amount. In the meantime, you can concentrate on other ways to make money. Based on the text you have in your page, it generates ads for you. In addition to image and text ads, it offers a Google search box. It also provides great way to make money from your website or blog.

You need to have a website or blog of your own to use AdSense money maker program. To get a free website, you can try Google Page Creator and for blogging you can try Blogger.com. Which is a good site to have Google AdSense ads?. It would be preferable to use AdSense money maker on a site that already has high traffic volume targeted towards it. Instead of designing a website for the sole purpose of using Google AdSense without useful content in it which will not drive good traffic, it is better to do it this way.

It is indeed possible to make good money with Google AdSense but you need to input lot of time and find out related categories for your website which pay high.

Chapter 7

The Benefits Of Creating Online Passive Income With Affiliate Programs

If you are looking to make money on the internet, affiliate programs are one of the best ways to start. There are many programs to choose from and you can begin today. Affiliate programs can be a great source of passive income for you. There are several types of income streams:

Linear Income is when we trade time for money. It is the way the majority of people are creating income for themselves. When you are paid for a set amount of time, usually 9-5, you are limited in your earning potential. If you are laid off, fired, ⏹uit you are not able to easily replace that income. And as we all know, there is no such thing as JOB security.

There is also the lack of personal freedom to consider. Are you a morning person? Or would you prefer later in the day? When is your most creative time? None of these things are considered when you are trading time for money. The majority of your waking hours are spent creating wealth for someone else.

Have you ever wanted to be able to take off for the day and be able to come and go as you please without having to check in with the boss, check to see if you have personal days, and worry about the pile up of work when you get back? There is another income source that can help provide more control over your income and lifestyle.

Passive Income is one of the better ways to create wealth and personal freedom for you and your family. Choosing the right affiliate program will help you make money daily, weekly, yearly. Working with an online business creates an unlimited opportunity to generate revenue. Your potential is only limited by your imagination. There are many affiliate programs that sell their products and service worldwide. This opens up a worldwide customer base for you. How exciting is it to make a sale and earn a make money right from the comfort of your own home and not have to worry about shipping, billing or packaging the product.

There has never been a better time than right now to take the first step to making money online with an affiliate program. The opportunities are unlimited and you are in the driver's seat.

Chapter 8

5 Tips on Earning Passive Income Online

1.Research -Make sure you know what you are getting into. Perform a Google search on the product, service, program you may be interested in. Check the forums, see what people are saying. If possible, check the Better Business Bureau to see if there have been any complaints and how they were resolved. Of course keep in mind, everyone will not be a happy camper.

2.Read the Fine Print - Did you read the fine print? Is this a one time charge? Monthly charge? Are there penalties of any sort? How much needs to be in your account before you receive a check? Read, read, read. If possible speak with someone on the phone to get your ⊡uestions answered.

3.Understand the Time Requirements - Making a passive income online is not easy in the beginning. You will have to research which methods will generate income (blogging, ebay, etc.) Do not be fooled by the word passive. Initial work is required, then the passive will fall into place. Set a few hours aside a day to work on your online ventures. The time you put in now, will pay off later.

4.Not Everything is a Scam - Yes, there are a lot of internet scams. Yes, there are a lot of sharks that will lie to you, take your money and run. But, you know what, that is not everybody, or every program online. If a particular program did not work for you, it just did not work for you. It does not mean it is a scam.

5.Set it on the Back Burner -It is OK to wait a while before investing time and/or money into a program. If the opportunity is legitimate, it will be there when you are ready. Do not fall for sales tactics and gimmicks, that play on a sense of urgency. Six months from now, the opportunity will still be there.

Chapter 9

Passive Income Online: Mistakes You Must Avoid

Here, you will explore about some mistakes and misconceptions about business models and how to avoid them.

These misconceptions may threaten your business model and destroy everything. You should note these factors while launching a business venture online. Do your homework, follow the warning signals and stay on track towards achieving the passive income-goal.

#1 Lack Of Research/Homework

If you're new in this business, you have to focus on making extensive research on the market, business prospect and the existing competition. You have to be precise about the facts and figures. You have to prepare your budget for the venture according to the research results. Lack of research won't let you initiate the cash flow even with the best passive income business idea. Take time and do your homework before you leap in.

#2 Lack Of Knowledge About The Model

There are different business models that can generate income for the business owner. Each business has its own terms, prospects and potentials. Online business models mostly follow a marketing principle that focuses on winning the leading search engines like Google, Yahoo and Bing. You have to learn about these basics before you launch the business online and start making money from it.

#3 The Most Popular Misconception Of 100% Income Generator

Most newbie entrepreneurs struggle with this misconception. People think a passive income business model will start generating money right away without any effort. But the truth is much different. Either you have to set up your own idea and populate the platform to reap profit. Or you can adopt a proven method and sync with an already running passive income maker. No matter what you choose, you have to put your effort in the beginning to start the cash flow.

#4 No Monitoring/Lack Of Maintenance

Once you have started making money from a passive business model, you have to make sure that the income flow is at a consistent level. You have to monitor the operation closely and regularly. You can use the advanced tool to run your online business without much manual operation. But you'll still need to monitor the progresses. At the same time, you have to consider making corrections whenever necessary.

Conclusion

For good reason, passive income is often considered to be the holy grail of investing, and the key to long-term wealth creation and wealth protection. The major benefit of passive income is that it is recurring income, typically generated month after month without a great deal of effort by you. Building wealth and becoming rich shouldn't be about extracting every last bit of your own energy, your own resources and your own money as there is always a limit to the extent you can do this. Tapping into the effective generation and use of passive income is a critical step on the road to wealth creation. Begin this part of you wealth creation journey as early as is humanly possible i.e. now!

Thank you again for purshising this book! I hope you have gotten adequate information and this book was able to help you start a refutable business online that guarantee passive income.

Finally, if you enjoyed this book, then I'd like to ask you for a favor, would you be kind enough to leave a review for this book on Amazon? It'd be greatly appreciated!

Check my other book here: JOB INTERVIEW: HOW TO SECURE AND GUARANTEE THE JOB. GUIDE TO PREPARE YOU TO LAND YOUR DREAM JOB.
MORE THAN 50 QUESTIONS TO ASSIST YOU FOR THE INTERVIEW

The key to success is to treat the interview as a project, for which you must gather information, make decisions on feasibility, set objectives, identify the resources needed, draw up a plan of action, and manage the project carefully through to closure. In simple terms, you must be professionally prepared for the interview, in order to have the optimum chance of success.

Showing up for a job interview can be pretty intimidating, especially when it's for a company that really interests you. There is nothing like sitting in the hot seat for an hour as your potential boss asks you every question under the sun.

The job interview is where you win or lose the offer. Even the world's best resume and cover letter won't save you if you commit common, critical mistakes. The REAL way to win an interview is by taking just a few extra steps before it even starts so you can craft the perfect answers, display high levels of competence, and get the job every time.

https://www.amazon.com/gp/product/B07WS2DLP3/

Thank you and good luck!